CAREERS FOR
HEROES

# SWAT TEAMS

**Anne Forest**

**PowerKiDS**
press.

New York

Published in 2016 by The Rosen Publishing Group, Inc.
29 East 21st Street, New York, NY 10010

First Edition

Editor: Katie Kawa
Book Design: Mickey Harmon

Photo Credits: Cover (SWAT man face) photo-nuke/Shutterstock.com; cover (SWAT uniform) Alex Studio/Shutterstock.com; cover (background) © iStockphoto.com/james Anderson; cover, pp. 1, 3, 4, 6, 8–9, 10, 12, 14, 16, 18, 20, 22–24 (gray and yellow textures) siro46/Shutterstock.com; pp. 5, 21 Boston Globe/Contributor/Boston Globe/Getty Images; p. 7 Kevork Djansezian/Staff/Getty Images News/Getty Images; p. 11 Geraldine Wilkins/Contributor/Los Angeles Times/Getty Images; pp. 13, 15, 17, 19 bibiphoto/Shutterstock.com; p. 16 Dave Navarro Jr/Shutterstock.com; p. 22 Oleg Zabielin/Shutterstock.com.

Cataloging-in-Publication Data

Names: Forest, Anne.
Title: SWAT teams / Anne Forest.
Description: New York : PowerKids Press, 2016. | Series: Careers for heroes | Includes index.
Identifiers: ISBN 9781508143987 (pbk.) | ISBN 9781508143994 (6 pack) | ISBN 9781508144007 (library bound)
Subjects: LCSH: Police–Special weapons and tactics units–Juvenile literature–United States.
Classification: LCC HV7922.F667 2016 | DDC 363.2'32–dc23

Manufactured in the United States of America

CPSIA Compliance Information: Batch #BW16PK: For Further Information contact Rosen Publishing, New York, New York at 1-800-237-9932

# CONTENTS

# SPECIAL WEAPONS AND TACTICS

Police officers face scary **situations** every day. However, some situations are too dangerous, or unsafe, for even the bravest police officer to face without special **weapons** and training. In these cases, special officers are called in to **protect** the public and their fellow members of the police force. These officers are members of SWAT teams.

"SWAT" stands for "Special Weapons and Tactics." Members of SWAT teams have learned to use weapons and tactics, or methods, to handle high-risk situations. Does a career as a SWAT team member sound interesting to you? Read on to learn more!

## FAST FACT!

Officers generally volunteer, or freely offer, to be part of a SWAT team. These volunteers know they're signing up for a dangerous—but very important—job.

SWAT team members are often easy to recognize because of their special gear. They wear different gear than other police officers because they need more protection.

# HOW SWAT TEAMS STARTED

SWAT teams weren't always a part of police departments in the United States. They started forming around the country in the 1960s and 1970s. SWAT teams served as an answer to the increasing **violence** that was hard for regular police officers to handle.

The Los Angeles Police Department (LAPD) was one of the first and most famous departments to start a SWAT team. In 1974, the LAPD SWAT team helped take down a dangerous **radical** group called the Symbionese Liberation Army (SLA). That helped show other police departments that SWAT team members could handle situations other officers weren't prepared to face.

## FAST FACT!

The LAPD SWAT team helped keep athletes and the public safe during the 1984 Summer Olympics, which were held in Los Angeles. Leaders of this SWAT team traveled to Europe before the Olympics to learn the best ways to prepare their officers for such a high-risk event.

SWAT teams in Los Angeles have faced many dangerous situations since the 1960s. Members of these SWAT teams continue to protect the millions of people who live in Los Angeles from dangerous and violent criminals.

# RISKY BUSINESS

SWAT teams are only called in to help with certain dangerous situations that other police officers aren't trained or **equipped** to face. SWAT teams often help other officers handle hostage situations, or situations in which a person is taken by someone against their will. SWAT teams also work to **resolve** situations in which a person is **barricaded** with a weapon.

SWAT teams can carry out raids on buildings known to house illegal drug or gang activity. They also serve warrants in high-risk places. A warrant is a document giving the police the right to search an area or arrest a person.

## FAST FACT!

A raid occurs when police officers, such as members of a SWAT team, forcefully enter a place to find drugs, weapons, or criminals. When a building is raided, criminals often violently fight back. This is why SWAT teams sometimes handle raids.

# Situations That Need SWAT Teams

**1**    hostage situations

**2**    barricaded subjects

**3**    suicidal subjects—people who want to kill themselves—who have a weapon

**4**    high-risk raids

**5**    high-risk warrants and arrests

**6**    crowd-control situations

**7**    visiting political leaders or other people who need special protection

These are some of the situations that SWAT team members might be called upon to handle. SWAT team members must be ready to face danger 24 hours a day, 365 days a year.

# SWAT TEAM SNIPERS

Different members of SWAT teams have different roles, or parts to play, on their team. They all need to work together to keep each other and the public safe.

A sniper is an important part of a SWAT team. It's the sniper's job to get close enough to see what's going on and report their findings to the rest of their team. A sniper is also trained to shoot a dangerous criminal if the criminal appears ready to take a life. Snipers train to shoot accurately, or without mistakes, from up close and very far away.

## FAST FACT!

SWAT team snipers go through long periods of testing and training before they can begin this career. They're tested on their shooting accuracy, as well as their physical and mental ability to handle such a hard job.

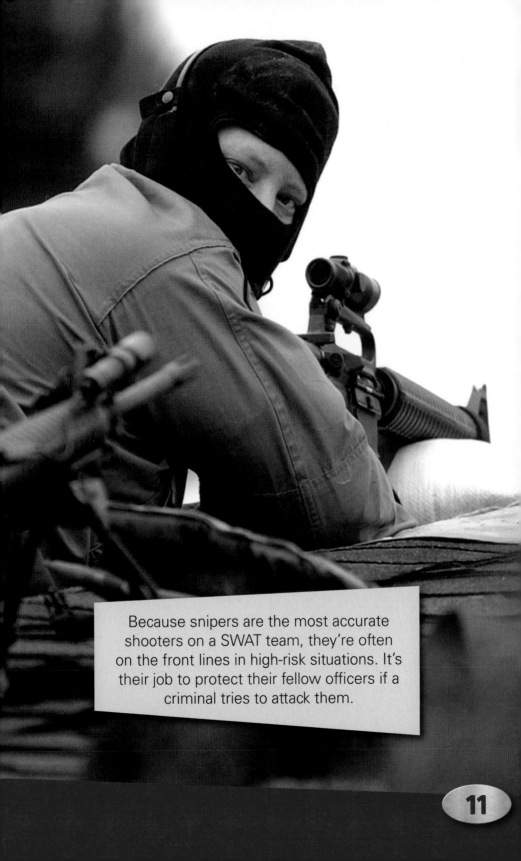

Because snipers are the most accurate shooters on a SWAT team, they're often on the front lines in high-risk situations. It's their job to protect their fellow officers if a criminal tries to attack them.

# THE ENTRY GROUP

While some SWAT team members are trained as snipers, others are trained as entry specialists, or members of an entry group. Their job is to enter a dangerous situation, such as a hostage situation or a building to be raided, and secure the **suspects**. They're also responsible for rescuing any other people, such as hostages, from those situations.

SWAT team members trained as entry specialists are taught to do whatever they can to avoid deadly violence. This sometimes means using certain **chemicals** that won't cause lasting harm in order to clear a building or stop a criminal.

## FAST FACT!

Some SWAT teams use robots as part of their entry group. A robot can do many tasks that could put SWAT team members in harm's way, including searching buildings for hostages and opening doors or windows with unknown dangers behind them.

SWAT team members are trained to enter situations that the rest of the public is told to stay far away from. You need to be very brave if you want to be part of a SWAT team!

# POWERFUL PROTECTION

SWAT team members have chosen a dangerous career. However, they use the most advanced equipment, or gear, to protect themselves. They wear sturdy boots, knee pads, and gloves. All SWAT team members also wear a helmet to protect their head and goggles to protect their eyes.

If you become a member of a SWAT team someday, you'll also wear a bulletproof vest. Some SWAT team members wear gas masks in case the air around them becomes toxic, or deadly. This could happen if a person put harmful chemicals into the air.

## FAST FACT!

Most SWAT teams use radios to communicate, or talk, with one another while they're working. Members talk into a microphone placed in the gear on their body, and they can hear each other through a special earpiece.

SWAT team members sometimes use a **shield** as an extra piece of protection. Much of the gear used by SWAT team members is similar to the gear used by members of the military.

# WEAPONS AND VEHICLES

The weapons used by SWAT team members are more powerful than those used by regular police officers. Their weapons need to be more powerful to face drug dealers and **terrorists** who have weapons capable of killing many people.

SWAT teams also have special vehicles, or machines used to move them from place to place. Many SWAT teams use armored vans or trucks. This kind of vehicle is covered with tough metal that can protect the people inside if the vehicle is attacked. SWAT teams also use helicopters in certain situations.

A SWAT vehicle is sometimes used as a mobile command center. This is a moveable place where leaders can oversee what their team is doing.

# FAST FACT!

A SWAT team can be called upon to stop a car carrying a dangerous person. Some SWAT team members are trained to use special driving techniques, or methods, to do this.

# BECOMING A SWAT TEAM MEMBER

Does being a member of a SWAT team sound like a career path you might want to follow? If it does, then you need to be prepared to go through a lot of training! Because SWAT teams work in high-risk situations, they need to be fully prepared before they start this job.

After going through physical, mental, and shooting accuracy tests to become a SWAT team member, the training starts. SWAT team members train to use the different kinds of equipment required for their job. They continue to train throughout their careers to keep their skills sharp.

## FAST FACT!

Not all SWAT team members work at this job full time. Many have other jobs in police departments, too, because situations that call for SWAT teams generally don't happen every day.

To become a SWAT team member, you'll need to serve as a police officer first. Most police departments only take volunteers that have at least three years of police experience, or time spent working as a police officer, for their SWAT teams.

# HEROES IN BOSTON

In communities around the United States, SWAT teams are used hundreds of times a year. Most of these cases don't make the national news, but in April 2013, SWAT teams working in Boston, Massachusetts, made headlines. They found and arrested a man who worked with his brother to set off two **bombs** at the Boston Marathon.

The SWAT teams went door to door in neighborhoods around Boston, looking for their suspect. Eventually, they found him hiding in a boat. Members of the SWAT teams surrounded the boat and arrested the man when he came out of hiding.

## FAST FACT!

SWAT teams from around Massachusetts worked with a SWAT team from the Federal Bureau of Investigation (FBI) to find and arrest the Boston Marathon bomber. SWAT team members need to be able to cooperate in order to be successful.

After the bombing of the Boston Marathon, the brave members of SWAT teams worked tirelessly to find the one bomber left alive. They used their special training to make Boston a safer place in a scary time.

# A SPECIAL KIND OF PERSON

SWAT teams are made up of brave people who want to keep their communities safe. It takes a special kind of person to join a SWAT team.

If you think you have what it takes to be a part of a SWAT team someday, then you can start preparing for this career now. SWAT team members have to be physically fit, so exercise every day. You should also continue to read as much as you can about this career. Maybe someday you'll be one of the heroes on a SWAT team, protecting people with your special skills!

# GLOSSARY

**barricade:** To block something so people or things are unable to enter or leave.

**bomb:** A device made to explode under certain conditions in order to hurt people or destroy property.

**chemical:** Matter that can be mixed with other matter to cause changes.

**equip:** To provide someone with the tools needed for a certain purpose.

**protect:** To keep safe.

**radical:** Having extreme political or social views that are not shared by most people.

**resolve:** To find an answer or solution to something.

**shield:** A large piece of metal carried by someone to keep them safe.

**situation:** All the facts, conditions, and events that affect someone or something in a certain time and place.

**suspect:** A person believed to be possibly guilty of committing a crime.

**terrorist:** A person who uses violence to scare people as a way of achieving a political goal.

**violence:** The use of physical force to cause harm.

**weapon:** Something used for fighting or attacking someone or fighting back when someone is attacking you.

# INDEX

# WEBSITES

Due to the changing nature of Internet links, PowerKids Press has developed an online list of websites related to the subject of this book. This site is updated regularly. Please use this link to access the list: www.powerkidslinks.com/chero/swat